VAISHNAVISM
OF THE
GOWD SARASWAT BRAHMINS
AND A FEW
KONKANI FOLKLORE TALES

amazon.in

Tax Invoice/Bill of Supply/Cash Memo
(Triplicate for Supplier)

Sold By :
Facsimile Publishers
C2/12 Pragati Market, Ashok Vihar Phase 2
NEW DELHI, DELHI, 110052
IN

PAN No: AAACG4699N
GST Registration No: NotApplicable

Billing Address :
Jaanvi
37-11-28/5, murali nagar,estate post, n.g.g.o.s colony
visakhapatnam, ANDHRA PRADESH, 530007
IN
State/UT Code: 37

Shipping Address :
Jaanvi
Jaanvi
37-11-28/5, murali nagar,estate post, n.g.g.o.s colony
visakhapatnam, ANDHRA PRADESH, 530007
IN
State/UT Code: 37
Place of supply: ANDHRA PRADESH
Place of delivery: ANDHRA PRADESH

Order Number: 407-8732935-3838768
Order Date: 03.12.2025

Invoice Number : IN-3976
Invoice Details : DL-132759261-2526
Invoice Date : 03.12.2025

Sl. No.	Description	Unit Price	Qty	Net Amount	Tax Rate	Tax Type	Tax Amount	Total Amount
1	Vishnavism of the Gowd Saraswat Brahmins and a Few Konkani Folklore Tales | 812124191X (PB1111021019863) HSN:49011010	₹130.00	1	₹130.00	0%	IGST	₹0.00	₹130.00
					0%	IGST	₹0.00	
					0%	None	₹0.00	
TOTAL:							₹0.00	₹130.00

Amount in Words:
One Hundred Thirty only

For Facsimile Publishers:

Authorized Signatory

Whether tax is payable under reverse charge - No

VAISHNAVISM
OF THE
GOWD SARASWAT BRAHMINS
AND A FEW
KONKANI FOLKLORE TALES

V. P. CHAVAN

GYAN

Published by

Gyan Publishing House
5, Ansari Road
Daryaganj, New Delhi-110002
Phone: 011-47034999, 9811692060
E-mail: books@gyanbooks.com

Distribution Network
gyanbooks.com
India, USA, Canada, UK, Australia, France

ISBN : 978-81-212-4191-5 (PB)
First Published, 1991

2nd Impression 2020

Printed at: Gyan Press, Delhi.

Vaishnavism of the Gowd Saraswat Brahmins and a Few Konkani Folklore Tales
Author: V. P. Chavan

VAISHNAVISM OF THE GOWD SARASWAT BRAHMIN SHAIVITES WITH SOME NOTES ON THE TWO SECTS OF VAISHNAVISM AND SHAIVISM.

India is a land of paradoxes, and Hinduism affords the most noted instance of that phenomenon. The philosophy, as developed in the Upanishads, has been considered the highest mark in hair-splitting logic but it shows us incidentally the powerful brains which threw illuminating light on those mystical problems trying to bring man nearer and nearer to the Almighty God.. Why "Self has to die", was the sum total of that philosophy. The philosophers fought against the common idea of "dust to dust, and ashes to ashes." Taking the soul as a spark from the Kindling Light, radiating from the *High above*, these Rishis fought and fought dogmatically to find the means to cross the bridge enabling the soul to get itself finally absorbed in the heavenly Effulgence. But these mighty Rishis wrote and talked over the heads of the common people and naturally lost touch with them. In his "Book of South India" Mr. J. C. Molony, I.C.S. (retired), aptly observes: "The ultimate speculations of the great Hindu thinkers, are interesting to the metaphysician but they are scarcely a guide and support to the average man in the daily perplexities of his life, in this world."

Man hankers after something—something personal, something adorable with a distinct personality, that should bring him in close touch with his God. The Hindu Philosophy soaring high up in the intellectual regions, was nothing but a floating dust with the common run of people. The elaborate and mechanical system of Vedic worship made us go in, in olden times, for all sorts of religious practices—practices which entailed human sacrifice, practices which made us go in for the serpent worship and the tree worship—practices which made even the intelligentsia bow down before the rituals used in the Tantric worship, which in ignorant hands, lapsed into even obscenities.

Hinduism has never been in the course of its whole history, a single organization. It has been allowed to grow wild like the weeds in jungles with an occasional flower sublime in its beauty and fragrant in its depth of learning, sprouting up here and there. Its philosophy has made it impractical. Hinduism is considered as a combination in fact of animism and pantheism. That is how the religion amongst the Hindus, as a vital force, is dead. The force round which all sorts of activities for the betterment of the masses, for the progressive uplift of the people, ought to have been centred, this vitality, this manifestation of energy, has practically never been born. That is why there is the eternal seeking for the betterment of *Self*, careless of the betterment of others.

That is where the saints came in. These men with super-human energies, with super-human abilities, tried and succeeded in giving a new direction to the worship of God as practised from time to time. The selfless sacred duty voluntarily undertaken, did leave the Indian world better from the religious point of view. They tried to blow that vitality into a flame, and succeeded to a certain extent. But the Boa-constrictor of mechanical rituals and sacrifices has always extinguished the flame and brought things to the dead level of old.

Both the Gods Shiva and Vishnu have excited a peculiar influence on the Hindus from times immemorial. The worship of God Shiva is known as "*Shaivism*". Some go to the extent of considering *Shiva*, not as an Aryan God. He is looked upon as the "Destroyer". He is called "Bhairava," *i.e.*, the fearful but all the same this deity is the life of the religious Soul of many millions in India. God Shiva is firmly rooted in our religious faith. He is described as the inconceivable one, who is beyond comprehension of all the Indian Gods.

The worship of God Shiva is considered the most aboriginal of the Indian cults as practised in the south of India where it flourished in about the 4th century B.C.* The worship of Rudra-Shiva was common to all during the Aryan period. But the worship of this deity, especially in the early Aryan period, was carried on with a sentiment of fear at the bottom. As Rudra was considered a terrible God, a wish was expressed in one's prayers that this evil spirit should be far, far away from the man who prayed to Him! The Linga worship had not come in use even at the time of Patanjali but the *Mahabharata* tells us that God Shiva is to be worshipped in the form of Linga, a phallic (B) symbol though usually decent in appearance.

The Vedas did not countenance this sort of worship. There is an allusion, however, in the Vedas (Rigveda) of Shishnadeva whom Indra was asked to destroy. God Shiva is said to batten upon corpses, and to smear his body with ashes from the burning ground.

* Emperor Asoka was a Shaiva (*Vide* Vincent Smith's Asoka—'Rulers of India' Series) and so were also his predecessors. In which case, it must have been a religion in vogue from at least the pre-Buddhistic times, in the North at least. If it had gone to the North, from the South, then it must have been, a living religion in the South, some centuries even earlier. *Vide* also Kalhana's राजतरंगिणी. I. verses 101—107.

(B) My friend Mr. M. Govind Pai believes that the Linga is not a phallic symbol but a representation of the digit one, indicative of Monotheism —एकमेवाद्वितीयम् and the पीठ or the stand on which it rests is not योनि (the female generative organ) but is indicative of Zero. From nothing, *i.e.*, from what can never be known, sprang God. The origin of God is therefore "unknowable." That is why he is called स्वयंभू.

Phallic worship was quite in vogue in Canaan (ancient Palestine or the country round about it), Phœnicia, &c. The reference to those whose God is "Shishna" (Bhandarkar's Vaishnavism, Shaivism, etc., p. 115) is perhaps to such people with whom our Vedic forefathers came into contact, but it may be that gradually, the phallic idea infiltrated into our ancient religion too, but in that case, it could only have the metaphorical significance of creative power.

God Shiva haunts mountains and deserted uncanny places. He is the patron of violent lawless men and robbers. In the play "Mrichchakatika" (6th century A.D.) a burglar invokes Kartikeya, the son of Shiva as the patron saint of thieves who is said to have taught different styles of house-breaking. God Shiva's neck is encircled by a serpent and a necklace of skulls.

The waves of Buddhism and especially Jainism checked the progress of *Shaivism*. The rebellion against ritualistic Hinduism, was carried on by Buddha in the first instance; but after all the victory rested with *Shaivism* on account of the tenets of the latter being regulated and strengthened by the flood of intellectual and philosophical current flowing from the Northern India. The revival of devotion, also due to the aggressive religious war carried on by a band of Sadhus and Acharyas, did away with the gross superstition and the demonolatry that was associated with the worship of God *Rudra-Shiva*. Finally the Shaivite schools of the Tamil country succeeded in rejecting the grosser elements and turned the worship of Shiva into an ecstatic and mystical monotheism.

A pure sincere devotion to God Shiva on the theistic basis took a strong hold on the public. It was about the twelfth century that Shaivism attained its high water mark all over India.

That is how God Shiva becomes the sole redeemer of souls. Redemption or the Moksha is the state of emancipation with a full conscious enjoyment of Shiva's presence. This shows the fervour of devotion leading to the doctrine of Grace. The Grace of God Shiva remains and He is still a personal deity but the individual self attains deliverance by being absorbed into the supreme and selfless one—God Shiva.

There is, however, some difference of Doctrine on this point. The soul becomes Shiva, equal to the Deity in power and knowledge, but still dependent on Him, rather than identical with Him.

The note of *Shaivism* has always been the unknowableness of God. The Advaita union with Lord Shiva is so complete that to those who obtained release, God Shiva will be all in all.

Shaivism possesses truth and force. The change which is the Law of Nature—produces, and destroys—reproduces and redestroys. This change manifests itself in fact in two aspects—beginning and an end. Shiva the destroyer, is in fact, the real creator of the world. It is on destruction that the process of growth is built up. You destroy the embryo and the child is born. You destroy the child and the man is born. Will there be any progress and improvement in the world inhabited by immortals only?

THE CULT OF VAISHNAVISM.

The cult of Vaishnavism on the other hand, has a continuous history even from before the beginning of the Christian era. The southern presidency was considered to be the stronghold of Shaivites; but in spite of all that, Vaishnavism managed to establish for itself a strong position there in about the eleventh century. There was not any keen antagonism between the Shaivites and the Vaishnavites at that time. Both the sects had a common basis to work up, *i.e.*, to uproot the prevalent Jainism from that part of the land.

Vaishnavism must be regarded as one of the most important religions of India. It was the religion of the Gupta Emperors, of Ramanuja, of Chaitanya, of Kabir, of Narasimha Mehta of Guzarat, and of our Tukaram also. It is the religion which produced the "Bhagawat Gita", and the songs of Tulsidas. The ideas of "Bhakti" and "Prasad"—Faith and divine grace—have been attributed to Vaishnavism.

According to Ray Chaudhuri—the well-known professor of the Calcutta University, Vaishnavism is the name given to the Bhakti religion which recognises Vishnu, who is also called Bhagwat, Narayan, Hari as the Sole God. Vishnu-worship is as old as Rig Veda. Vishnu is considered as one of the Adityas or manifestations of the Sun. He was considered not a great God in the earliest Vedic times. There may be a good deal of truth[1] in Grierson's surmise that the Bhagwat Doctrine was a development of the sun worship that was the common heritage of both branches of the Aryan people—the Iranian and the Indian. There are records testifying to the proselytising zeal of the Bhagwatas in the pre-Christian centuries which show that their religion was excellent and persuasive enough to capture the hearts of cultured Greeks and catholic enough to admit them into its fold. The Greek Heliodoros calls himself a Bhagwata in an inscription recorded on the column found at Besnagar and supposed to date from the first part of the second century B.C. God Vishnu's real claim to reverence is due to the fact that certain popular incarnations and *Krishna* are identified with him. The worship of the ever popular Rama has become a watch-word of Hinduism.

Bhâgavata (possibly from भग one of the primitive Aryan deifications) means worshipper of the one Lord. Bhâgawat Dharma was also called "Ekantika Dharma" or the religion with one object, *i.e.*, monotheism.[2]

---

1. Later considerations have however, compelled me to change my views. If Mr. Grierson be right, we must expect to find, in that case, something similar to the pure "Bhakti-Marga" in Avestan religion; but is there anything there like the Vaishnava Bhaktimarga? No! For the most religious of the least ritualistic of the Avestan literature, *viz.*, the Gathas have scarcely anything like our Bhakti literature. They are more or less like the Hebrew Psalms of the Old Testament. Nor do their "Nyaishes" containing hymns to "Mithra," &c., disclose anything, similar to our Bhakti-marga. (*Vide* 'Nyaishes' edited by Dr. Dhalla; Gathas with Guzerathi Translation by Kanga and the English translation of the Gathas in the *S. B. E.* Series, Vol. XXXI, by Mills.)

2. Historically speaking, the Jain Dharma was founded by Mahavir who seems to have died in 527 B.C. Now the Jainism is called the अनेकान्त (anekanta) religion. (जैनोनेकान्तवाचपि–अभिधान चिंतामणि शिलोञ्छ: p. 3 verse 76 in the work called अभिधानसंग्रह). It goes without saying that there could never be an अनेकान्त unless or until there was an एकान्त (in contradiction to it) flourishing long before it. Wherefore, it follows that the एकान्तिक भागवत धर्म must have originated at least a century or two before the genesis of Jainism, *i.e.*, before 527 B.C.

Bhâgawata from Bhagawân—

"Bhag" + wân = Possessing "भग"

ऐश्वर्यस्य समग्रस्य वीर्यस्य यशसः श्रियः ।

ज्ञानवैराग्ययोश्चैव षण्णां "भग" इतीरणा ॥

Vaishnavism teaches one to go in for personal devotion rendered to a personal God. The lower classes to whom the ambiguities of Vedantism and the hair-splitting obscurities of the theologian and the philosopher, were too much, readily accepted a cult which opened an easy way of salvation by Bhakti or devotion.

Vaishnavism fought against the spiritual monism and Maya, or the world illusion, that was promulgated by Shree Shankaracharya. Ramanuja unfurled the banner of Bhakti and the battle was carried on by his successor Madhvacharya who brought into prominence God Vishnu as the Supreme God.

My friend, Mr. Govind Pai of South Canara, informs me that he is constrained to differ from this view. He says, the first Shankaracharya was as much devoted to Vishnu as to Shiva, as evidenced by so many of his works. He identified them with one another and took them as only the two different aspects of the same God-head.

Mr. G. Pai further observes that Madhvacharya was never a disciple of, nor even a follower of Ramanuja or his school. He founded quite a different school altogether. His idea of the worship of Vishnu was quite different from that of Ramanuja. According to Madhva, "Vayu" is the mediator between us and God. Whereas according to Ramanuja there is no such mediator and the attainment is direct. Next, Madhva was more attached to Krishna, whereas Ramanuja was to Rama.

Would any body believe that Vaishnavism even in those days spelt democracy pure and simple? The Alwars or the Tamil saints carried on the worship in their temples in the Tamil language. The great Ramanuja was ever alert to unfold to the common masses in simple language the rudiments of his faith and conviction. Vedic texts were translated into Tamil and were and are still being sung in the Vedic intonation in Ramanuja Temples in the South. This brings to our mind the great and sturdy simplicity of saint Tukaram, who succeeded in a marvellous way like Ramanuja the great, in making the shrine of "*Vithoba*" of Pandharpur, as the source of salvation not only to the ignorant kunbi, but to the intelligent Brahmin as well. The depressed "Mahar" and the "Mochee" are to be found in the annual crowd who visit the shrine. The Mahar Saint Chokha has a prominent place given to his image in the Temples at Pandharpur. The beauty of saint Tukaram's teaching was such that even a Mahomedan or two were and even now are to be occasionally found in the crowd praying to God Vithoba.

The pure Bhakti of Vithoba is nothing but a local manifestation of the cult of devotion carried on by Ramanuja and his successors, centuries and centuries ago before saint Tukaram was born.

There appears to be a "Pandurang Stotra" by Shankaracharya, and if that be genuinely his, the Vithoba worship must have been in vogue long before Ramanuja. (Shankara 9th centuary A.C. and Ramanuja *circa* 12th century).

Tukaram prayed to God Vithoba, sang to Vithoba, and dreamt of Vithoba. In fact, such was his religious fervour with which he identified himself with the attributes of God Vithoba that he got himself thoroughly saturated with the unselfish devotion to God Vithoba.

In a letter to Shivaji, who desired to see him, Tukaram wrote "as a chaste wife longs only to see her Lord, such am I to Vithoba. All the world to me is Vithoba and nothing else. Thee also I behold in Him."

The spirit of pure devotion or Bhakti is to be found in the followers of Vaishnavism. The spirit of sympathy for the lower castes and classes of Hindu Society has been a distinguishing feature of Vaishnavism. Ramanuja was noted for his largeness of heart. Ramanuja did away with the caste system by accepting a Non-Brahmin as a Guru. Ramanuja himself treated Tirukka-Cacinambi, a Shudra disciple of Alavandar, as his teacher. After his bath, Ramanuja would invariably take for his support Pillai Urangavalli Desar, a Shudra. Even people belonging to the depressed Panchama caste were not excluded from the religious teaching. But there is one difference between Ramanuja and Ramananda. Ramanuja admitted into his immediate circle, those, who could follow him in his dissertations on Upanishads and Vedanta philosophy, thus limiting the number, especially of the Shudras. While with Ramananda, the case was otherwise, as will be explained later on.

Theism as unfolded by Ramanuja is based on Vedanta Philosophy and relies on pure Bhakti or the loving faith of the worshipper, for one's salvation. Bhakti is also defined as a passionate self-oblivious devotion to a deity. There is no question that Vaishnavism owed its popularity to the emotional warmth which Ramanuja was able to infuse into his doctrines. Vaishnavism is called the Bhâgwat Dharma because it succeeded in completing the work of the Bhagwat Geeta in Indian Theism, under the Great Ramanuja.* This saint was followed by Shree Madhvacharya [a] about a century later, who established the *Dwaita* system. This insists on Bhakti as the only way of salvation procuring deliverance from the bondage of "*Samsara*" and endows one with a life of bliss and perfection in the presence of God. God can only be approached through a mediator.† The grace of God is to be had only if there be perfect faith in the follower or seeker.

---

* It will be interesting to know that the term Bhâgawat was in vogue some fourteen centuries before Ramanuja from the following inscription: "देव देवस वासुदेवस गरुडध्वजे अयं कारिते हेलिओदोरेण भागवतेन."

(a) Shree Madhvacharya was not a follower of Ramanuja, nor a dissenter from the latter but an independent founder of quite a new school.

† In this aspect, it comes closest of all Indian religious systems to Christianity.

Madhvacharya insisted on the sovereignty of God holding that it is the divine grace that sets men free, so it is the divine will that has cast them into bondage. The saint Madhvacharya was against the sacrifice of animals and recognised the religious rites of all classes of the people. But this Acharya introduced the spirit of intolerance especially against the monistic interpretations of the universe.

Madhvacharya is supposed to have put on a different meaning altogether on a well-known saying in the *Chhandogya Upanishad* "*Sa Atma tat tvam asi*". It is said that he forced into this text a sense of an opposite nature, a meaning consistent with his own special doctrine. This Acharya rendered this text into "*Sa atma atat tvam asi*" meaning "you are not that God. Why be so conceited as to suppose that you are"!

It is Shree Madhvacharya and his immediate successors that introduced Vaishnavism among the Gowd Saraswat Brahmins. I cannot help mentioning here how Vaishnavism at one time was run on the most broadened democratic basis. Shree Ramananda who flourished at about the beginning of the 15th century went full tilt against the water-tight caste system amongst the Hindus. This saint established a "*Matha*" (monastery) in Benares on the cosmopolitan principle of "No caste, no creed". "Whosoever adores God, he is God's own". It is no wonder therefore, that he had a Mahomedan weaver, a mochee, a barber, amongst his apostles. The democracy for which the Vaishnavism fought and bled, reached its zenith under the all-pervading influence of Ramananda. Whatever idol was worshipped within the pantheon of Vaishnavism, there flowed around it the continuous stream of the River of Bhakti. The water of *faith and love* is the one and the only one way, by which the inner stain, the sins of omission and commission can ever be effaced.

In the "Rise of the Maratha power", the late Mr. Justice Ranade says:—"The Bhakti of Vithoba modified the

" strictness of the old spirit of caste exclusiveness. It raised
" the Shudra classes to a position of spiritual power
" and social importance almost equal to that of the Brahmin.
" Mutual toleration was established. It suggested and partly
" carried out a plan of reconciliation with the Mahomedans.
" It subordinated the importance of rites and ceremonies, &c.,
" to the higher excellence of worship by means of *Love* and
" *Faith*. It checked the excesses of polytheism. It tended
" in all these ways to raise the nation generally to a higher
" level of capacity both of thought and of action"

In short the idea underlying Vaishnavism is human and emotional. God Vishnu asks for worship through *love*. Shaivism on the other hand makes one tread in the scientific and philosophic currents rather than in the emotional ones. Both the forms of worship seek for deliverance from transmigration. The two forms of worship co-existed in remote periods, not as we find them now. But in their higher phases, both the sects arrive at similarly excellent religious points, though through different channels. Both provide the strength necessary to accomplish self-effacement, and attain renunciation.

A good story is told of Shree Shankaracharya [a] popularly supposed to be the founder of Shaivism. His real religion was

(a) Mr. M. Govind Pai informs me however that Shaivism had long been in existence before the times of Shankaracharya and the latter should not be considered as the founder of it. Shree Shankaracharya is no doubt popularly believed to be the founder of the *Advait* system but here also Mr. Pai rightly insists that one finds the philosophy of *Advait* in the works of Gowd Padacharya, who was the Paramaguru (his teacher's teacher) of Shankaracharya. The Upanishads such as the Svetasvatar, etc. discuss the doctrines of Advaitism. Under historical research, one is sorry to see that "popular idols" are broken. All the same it must never be forgotten that Shankaracharya himself has done so much for the propagation of *Bhakti* too. (*Vide* so many of his "stotras" especially his very famous

षट्पदी—

" सत्यपिभेदापगमे नाथ तवाहं न मामकीनस्त्वम् ।
" सामुद्रो हि तरंगः क्वच न समुद्रो न तारंगः ॥

Vedantism—Advaitism. The legend says that when summoned to his mother's death bed, he spoke to her first of the Vedanta philosophy. But when she bade him give her some consolation which she could understand, he recited a hymn to *Shiva* but when the attendants of that God appeared, she was frightened. Shankaracharya then recited a hymn to Vishnu and when his gentler messengers came to her bedside, the old mother felt a thrill of satisfaction and she blessed her son and her soul wafted away to *Vaikuntha*—the heavenly home of *God Vishnu*!

This looks like a story invented by the intolerant Vaishnavas to ridicule Shankaracharya [a] but it throws decidedly a strong light on the way, in which an ordinary man with ordinary intelligence goes in for that school of thought or worship which is most understandable, easy to follow and is free of all rituals. I mean the Bhakti or the school of personal devotion. The worship of God Shiva coupled with Vedantism and with Smritis is on the other hand too difficult a nut for the ordinary lay mind to crack. That is why Vaishnavism associated with such eminent names as Ramanuja and Ramananda, Nrisimha Mehta, Chaitanya, Tukaram, and Kabir, has influenced all India.

THE INTOLERANCE OF THE VAISHNAVAS.

As I have already mentioned both the sects—the followers of *God Shiva* and *God Vishnu*—carried on their activities side by side in a peaceful manner. The common enemy, in the South, the Jainism had to be destroyed. But with the decadence of the latter, the natural animosities burst asunder. A large following especially from the uncultured classes went in for *Vaishnavism*. The Shaivites were up in arms. So much so that one of the kings, called the *Chola* king *Kurattâl*, sent an urgent summons to *Ramanuja*, the great apostle of *Vaishnavism*. Apprehending danger to his *Guru*, *Vân* a disciple put on the Sanyasi's garb and impersonated his teacher in

a See footnote (a) in page 11.

the King's presence. On being questioned if he had any objections to subscribe to the faith of *Shaivism*, and to repeat that "There was none superior to *God Shiva*", the *Vaishnavite* disciple replied impertinently that *Drona* was bigger than *Shiva*, playing upon the words *Shiva* and *Drona*—two measures of which *Drona* was bigger.

शिवात्परतरं नास्ति ।

द्रोणमस्ति ततः परम् ॥

For this, that Vaishnavite disciple had to suffer—his eyes were put out by the king's orders, then and there.

Perhaps these pinpricks and occasional persecutions must have made the lot of the followers of *Ramanuja*, very hard in the beginning. But as the worship of *God Vishnu* went on gathering strength not only in numbers but in religious fervour also, a condition grew up which made people look upon the *Shaivites* with no uncertain measure of hatred and enmity. That hatred, that enmity, has been handed down, to the present generations even, after a lapse of so many centuries. The *Shaivites* have now cooled down. They look upon *Vaishnavism* as a necessary evil to be put up with, in silence. But the flame of intolerance burning in the breast of Vaishnavites, continues to glow with unabated fury and violence even at the present day.

The first thing that strikes one is the sectarian mark on the forehead. The *Smartas* or the *Shaivites* put the mark with a horizontal line parallel with the eyebrows. The *Vaishnavites* go in for a straight perpendicular mark which ends to a point between the eyebrows. In the case of *Tengalais*,[a] a sub-sect of *Ramanuja's Vaishnavism*, this straight mark is prolonged down to the tip of the nose. The Vaishnavites reject sacrifice in toto,

(*a*) The Tengalais who are Southerners put the mark in a Y-shaped fashion whereas that of the Vadgalais (*i.e.* the Northerners of Ramanuja persuasion) is V. shaped.

the basis of salvation in their case being emotional fervour When bowing before their *Gods*, the Vaishnavites stand straight before their *idol*, join both the hands together, place them before the nose and bow down. As all this means a straight line, the sectarian mark of the followers of *God Vishnu*, the *Shaivite* after joining his hands and placing them before his nose, does not stand straight facing the *Gods*. He turns his face sideways and bows down that way—this pose can easily be interpreted into a horizontal line. Even in scrubbing the dirty pots, the *Vaishnavite* lady does so in an up and down, and up and down manner. The *Shaivite* one scrubs it from side to side and never in an up and down manner. Shaivites will sit for their dinners in a line so that all can face their idols—which means in a line parallel with their idols suggesting the horizontal mark again. The *Vaishnavites*, on the other hand, will arrange and place their plates at right angles to the idol, and this means the straight line. A sub-sect of the *Vaishnavas* called *Kadaka*(b) *Vaishnavas* carry their intolerance still further. They use a wet cloth when taking their meals. The *Shaivites* along with other Brahmins, are in the habit of changing their cotton Dhotees for those of silk or other material, which are only to be worn at the time of meals, a sort of dinner pants. The *Kadaka Vaishnavas* will not dine off a metal plate but will use plantain or other suitable leaves for the purpose. Some other old orthodox *Kadaka Vaishnavas* go so far as to go to the extent of purifying themselves by a bath, if they happen to come across a *Shaivite Brahmin* especially immediately before their meals. Even the mere sight of *Shaivite Brahmin* is considered impure and lessening one's chances of a *Moksha* salvation.

On the *Maha Shivaratri* day, the day of all the days from the *Shaivite* point of view, when a strict fast is observed in honour of *God Shiva* by his followers, these *Kadaka Vaishnavas* will go

---

(b) This is not exactly a name but a facetious way of calling them. The correct word is *Kadu Vaishnava*. *Kadu*, a Canarese word, equivalent to Sanskrit word *Ati*, means "hard."

in for full feasting. They will prepare special sweet dishes just to show their malicious neglect and hatred of that deity. On account of inter-marriages between these two sects among the *Gowd Saraswatas*, the Vaishnavite husband is obliged, many a time to fast on a *Maha Shivaratri* and other similar holidays on account of his Shaivite wife going in on a strike, on those days and observing a strict fast. The result being that it is the wife who sets the tune in the family harmonium in such cases. The *Tulsi* plant is supposed to be a favourite plant of *God Vishnu*. On the 12th day of the bright half of Kartika, the *God Vishnu* gets married to the *Tulsi plant*. That is why these Vaishnavites masticate a leaf or two of the *Tulsi* plant before or after their meals. Some of the *Vaishnavites* even wear the leaf rolled up in the lobe of their right ears. The hallmark of *Vaishnavism* is to get oneself branded on the temples and on the different parts of the body with the stamps bearing the impressions of the four weapons of *God Vishnu*, the conchshell, the discus, the mace, and the lotus (Shankha, Chakra, Gada and Padma) and a square stamp called Narayan so called from its nine squares being fitted with *Narayan Ashtakshar* mantra ॐ नमो नारायणाय. The straight mark on the forehead is painted with a bit of charcoal. The *Shaivites* on the other hand, never use a coal but go in for a sandal wood paste. To sew a coat is translated in Marathi as शिवणें but the Vaishnavite is not prepared to use the letters शिव and he asks his tailor therefore to get his coat वैष्णवुन हेणें. The *Smartas* use holy ashes for marking the various parts of the body and their women follow their husbands by putting the 'kunkuma for their tilak in a horizontal streak along the forehead. The Vaishnavites use 'Gopichandan' a sort of white clay instead of ashes for marking the body with the caste sign. Their women mark their heads vertically with kunkuma made of turmeric mixed with chunam. The term of reproach for a *Vaishnavite* on the part of a *Smarta* is that the former is called तो सामको उभो गीरे ! meaning that "he is nothing but a bundle of perpendicular and meaningless lines". In certain parts of Karwar, men and women washing their clothes and beating them on the stones, say "Shau shau" every time the cloth is beaten against the stone, the Vaishnavite thinking that this "Shau shau" approximates in pronunciation to Shiva, particularly avoid saying it, but say Hâ, Hâ !!

After the worship is over, a Vaishnavite will say कृष्णार्पणमस्तु and the Shaivite will give utterance to ब्रह्मार्पणमस्तु.

The Times are changing. There is the idea, the spirit of Nationalism abroad. The intolerant spirit is getting less and less. This is much more true in the case of the Gowd Saraswat Brahmins, as may be found later on in this paper.

THE GOWD SARASWAT BRAHMINS.

Before I proceed further I would like to make one thing clear. These Gowd Saraswat Brahmins are termed the *Smartas*. They are not exactly *Shaivites*. As I have already shown that the great Shankaracharya, not only fought for *Advaitism* but went in for *Bhakti* also. His followers, especially those belonging to the G. S. Brahmins, are known as *Smartas*. They pay an equal homage, not only to *Shiva* and *Vishnu* but also to Durga, Ganpati and the Sun, so much so that their worship is called a पंचायतन worship—worship of the five Gods. They worship *Shiva* and *Vishnu* with equal devotion but the "Naivedya"—the food offering is performed by them only to the latter, as according to Puranic traditions, on account of a curse from Bhrigu upon *Shiva*, his 'Naivedya' is unacceptable. Shankaracharya himself was called a षण्मतप्रतिष्ठापनाचार्य (the establisher of the six creeds, Shaivism, Vaishnavism, Shākta, Gánapatya, Skānda and Saura creeds) and he established temples for all these six creeds at Shringeri in Mysore, where his principal *Math* is still in existence. In every *Smarta* temple, as also in every *Smarta* house, whenever there is a family God, there the Saligram stones, representatives of Vishnu, besides a Linga of Siva, even if there be no images of the former, are to be found. The so-called *Shaiva* section of the Gowd Saraswats, is really a *Smarta* persuasion. Their Guru, the Kavale-math Swami is a Smarta Sanyasi and it is known on reliable authority that among the images of his own every day worship are, not only the Linga of Bhawani Shankar but also the images of Muralidhar, besides the Saligram stones and it is to the Vishnu idols, *i.e.* the Saligrams, that he offers the daily Naivedya, which he partakes of afterwards. So the appellation *Shaiva* as applied to the *Smartas* or to any other section which plays an equal homage to Vishnu, is quite misleading, if not actually wrong. The *Smarta* in fact looks upon "Hari and Har" with equal devotion and considers them as two different aspects of the same God.

A little account of the history of these decidedly clever and intelligent Gowd Saraswat Brahmins, is necessary to show the place they held, not only as *Vedic* scholars but as Brahmin priests, who were thoroughly conversant with the difficult *Vedic* rituals in the early centuries before the Christian era. It is said (*Vide* Sahyadri-Khand and Sūta Samhita) that *Shree Parashuram*, one of the incarnations in the Hindu Mythology brought from Trihotrapur, Brahmins of ten Gotras belonging to this community and settled them in a province which is known now as Goa. Other batches followed and a large colony was established. The terrible *Parashuram*, the Brahmin of the Brahmins, who is said to have waged perpetual wars with the *Kshatriyas* for political domination, would have been the last man to select any class of Brahmins who were not considered the best scholars of the times. These *Saraswat Brahmins* migrated in course of time to the fertile lands of Videha in Northern Bihar and settled in Trihotrapur in Mithila. The ancient name of this central part was *Gowd* and so it followed that they were known as *Gowd Saraswat Brahmins.*

The Shatapatha Brahman gives a good account in its 1st Khand, 4th Chapter of one of the earliest migrations of these Brahmins from the banks of the Saraswati river towards the East to Videha. I believe this is the earliest historical migration of the remote ancestors of these Gowd Saraswat Brahmins from their original home towards the East—if one believes, according to the Puranic traditions, that it was from Tirhut that Parashuram got them to settle down in Goa. The Saraswatakhyan in the Gadaparva of the Maha Bharat gives us, also, an account of another very early migration, which was perhaps directly from the banks of the Sarasvati on to the west coast of the Sahyadris. In that case, this must be another migration—quite a different one from the other migration, described in the Shatapatha.

There is a great probability that these Brahmins had to leave Videha on economic grounds. Mithila became the headquarters of Buddhism by the time, Sanskrit had lost its influence as the *lingua franca* and got broken up into countless Prâkrit dialects. The rise of Buddhism moreover considerably loosened the bonds of the old religion of Brahminism with its innumerable rituals, sacrifices, etc. In fact it gave a deadly blow to ritualism. The Saraswat Brahmins were past masters in all these intricate ceremonies and they lived and maintained themselves on that. But the check which the Buddhism gave to Brahminism, especially the principle of *Ahimsa*—"Killing is Sin"—made the great sacrifices fall into disuse. Vedic scholarship which was essentially necessary for the careful performance of the sacrifices, must have got to be a superfluous commodity on the market. Consequently the means of subsistence for these Brahmins was evaporated and that is why the great trek to the fertile fields of the Konkan took place.

That is how these Brahmins thoroughly saturated with Vedantism looked upon the Vedas as the highest scriptural authority. As already mentioned, the worship of God Shiva was prevalent under one name or other in the early centuries of the Christian era. There is a bold surmise that Buddha and his followers were really responsible for the growth of image worship. Dr. Bhandarkar and Rameshchandra Dutt have been of opinion that the spread of idol worship was due to Buddhism. Sermons and meditation were very well, for the Buddhistic monks, brought up under strict control but for the ordinary laity, the illiterate masses, it was too indigestible a morsel to swallow. A strong reaction took place and the people went in for some outward form of worship. The worship of God Shiva and the demonolatry with which it was associated at first, captured the imagination of the masses in general. Kalimata with her fearful sacrifices, was nothing but an appetiser to the starved religious minds of the people in those times. The Gowd Saraswat Brahmins had to fall in line and went in for the worship of God Shiva. But the basis of their faith was the recognition of that great body of Indian Traditions known as the Smritis. And this, next to Vedantism was the essence of the great Shankaracharya's teaching. Because they believed in the Smritis, the Gowd Saraswat Brahmins are called the Smartas.

गौर, गौळ or गौड though once restricted as the name of a certain district, came gradually to be used for a large provincial tract including बंग, पौण्ड्र, &c., and the designation "Gowd" was perhaps used by the Southerners in an extensive sense, comprising all the Northern Brahmin communities living in those districts. But all the same, it is a wonder how the Saraswats, colonised in Videha (Mithila) came to be known as "Gowd" Saraswats, which is clearly and historically a misnomer. (a) Perhaps they were thought to be closely connected with their Gowd

---

(a) The northern Brahmins are called Panch-gowdas and the Southerners as Panch-dravids, but both of these names are pure and simple misnomers. The correct way of saying these names is (1) गौडादि पंचविध ब्राह्मणाः and (2) द्राविडादि पंचविध ब्राह्मणाः i. e. (1) the five classes of Brahmins beginning with गौड (i. e., गौड, सारस्वत, कान्यकुब्ज, मैथिल and उत्कल) and (2) the five classes of Southern Brahmins beginning with द्राविड (i. e. द्राविड which is the wrong and corrupt form of द्रामिल from द्रमिलदेश, a Tamil country, Ptolemy's Damurica, आन्ध्र i. e., Telagu, कर्णाटक, महाराष्ट्र and गुर्जर). Now as the name Saraswat, wherever the five Northern Sections are mentioned in Puranas or elsewhere, occurs always next to 'Gowd', it came to be closely and indissolubly associated with it and though history has no warrant for it, came to be known as the Gowd Saraswates; a .. also instead of saying गौडादि पंचविध ब्राह्मणाः, all the Northerns came to be called in the South as the Panch Gowds. In Orissa, the Utkal Brahmins, a section of the Panch Gowds, call themselves Utkal Gowd Brahmins! A parallel instance may be quoted. Even now, all the Southern Brahmins are called the Dravidas, though this is the name of only one class of Brahmins known as द्राविडादि पंचविध ब्राह्मणाः (Mr. M. Govind Pai.)

bretheren (one of the five divisions of the Gowd Brahmins) than with their Maithila bretheren. One thing is certain, the word Gowd Saraswat must have been applied to them, after their immigration to the South, by the Southerners. For this word "Gowd Saraswat" has never been used or even applied to them in the North. There these Gowd Saraswat Brahmins are known merely as Saraswats, all throughout the Kashmir and the Punjab, the U. P. and the Bengal.

Shree Shankaracharya gave a great impetus to the principles of Vedantism, etc., coupled with the worship of God Shiva. He overthrew the tottering forces of Buddhism and naturally the Gowd Saraswat Brahmins came under his influence and sway. The worship of God Shiva and his various Godlings occupied the chief place in the minds of that community and the use of Vedic rituals gradually fell into decay.

It must be mentioned here, however that so far as traditions can be relied upon, the Kavale math Swami traces his descent from Gowdapada Acharya, who was a Gowd Brahmin and who was the "parama guru" of Shree Shankaracharya. The descent can be summarised as under :—

गौडपादाचार्य

- विवरणानंद सरस्वति
  - कवळे मठ
- गोविंद यति
  - शंकराचार्य
    - शृंगेरी मठ
    - द्वारका मठ
    - बद्री मठ
    - गोवर्धन मठ पुरी (ओरिसा)

The Swamis of all the four maths of Shankaracharya, even now add the title "Shree Shankaracharya" to their names; whereas the Kavalemath Swami's standing title is "Gowda padacharya." So the Advaitism adopted by the ancestors of the Gowd Saraswats must be traced to the source of Gowda padacharya, if not still earlier, though it may have received a large, a very large impetus, later on from Shankaracharya.

That is why Vaishnavism with all its pushfulness, its aggressiveness, its simplicity, has not succeeded in driving away that sense of real comfort, that sense of real peace from the religious and cultured minds of this great community, which they have found in the old worship of their old Gods of the Shaivite sect.

I have already mentioned that Shree Madhvacharya was the first saint who introduced Vaishnavism into the Gowd Saraswat Brahmins. (Vide Madhva-Vijaya Canto X)

The Gowd Saraswat Brahmins had to migrate to the Cochin and Travancore side, during the Portuguese † persecutions, but some of the old and informed leaders of this community assure me that in about the 13th century there was also an influx of Gowd Saraswat Brahmins to this side on account of Mahomedan persecution. Madhvacharya was in the zenith of his fighting power. The Konkani Brahmins as they were called differed naturally from the local Brahmins not only in dress, customs, manner and habits, etc., but what was worse in religion as well. The Konkani Brahmins were Shaivites and the local religion was Vaishnavism in its aggressive mood. These Saraswatas were allowed to stay there only after they had agreed to the conditions laid down by the Travancore authorities. These conditions are humorously described as :—

अन्नस्य पिंडम् । वस्त्रस्य तुंडम् ।
सर्वांग मुंडम् । मलबार भण्डम् ॥

Our friends, the Parsee community, had to accept similar conditions when they were allowed to settle in India. There

---

† M. Govind Pai informs me that the last and general exodus of the Gowd Saraswats took place from Goa in and after 1510 A.D. So far it can be ascertained, the earliest Temple, the Gowd Saraswats founded in South Kanara, was at Karkal in 1537 A.D.

was one gentleman called Narayan who was the leader of the Gowd Saraswatas. Madhvacharya worked his persuading powers on him and made him a disciple of his. There is a copper plate of Shaliwahan Shaka 1404, regarding this important conversion. From the Kavya 'Madhva Vijayam,' we understand that the Saraswat Brahmins of Goa were all Smartas before the advent of Shree Madhva and were followers of the Kaivalypura math of the monastic order styled after Gowd Padacharya. The great Shankaracharya was the disciple of Govindayati, the disciple of Gowda Padacharya.

It is said that Narayan was taken by Madhvacharya on a pilgrimage to Badrinath. Narayan got very ill. He was turned into a Sanyasi, more with the idea of saving the botheration of funeral pyre. A sanyasi's body is thrown into the river Ganges after his death and there the matter ends. But strange to relate, Narayan recovered. Fortunately for him, there were no doctors. Narayan was grateful to his Guru. He was asked in return, to go back to Gomantak and work there to spread the knowledge of Vaishnavism amongst his community.

That might be one of the ways, Vaishnavism was introduced but all accounts agree that it was Madhvacharya who spread the worship of God Vishnu among the Gowd Saraswatas. The portions of Goa, known as Bardes and Salcete were converted whole sale to the new sect. The names Sasastikars and Bardeshkars, mean literally the inhabitants of these places; but they have come to mean in popular parlance, those Gowd Saraswat Brahmins who have accepted Vaishnavism.

There is another account. In the year 1475 A.C. (according to the Guru paramparamritam, canto I verses 26-27) a Gowd Saraswat Brahmin named Madhav was initiated and ordained a Sanyasi with the name of Narayanatirtha at Badrinath by a Dravid Swami called Ramachandratirtha of Palimaru Math, one of the eight monasteries established at Udipi in South Canara by Madhvacharya. It is from this Narayantirtha that the Swamis of the Gokarna or Partagali math of the G. S. Brahmins, trace their descent and therefore even now these latter Swamis and especially the G. S. Vaishnavas pay some homage to the Swamis of Palimarumath. It is said that Madhvacharya himself never ordained any Sanyasis from the Gowd Saraswatas living in Goa. When he visited Goa, he got a large number of followers there, especially as he was not at all opposed to the worship of Shiva also. That is why the Gowd Saraswat Brahmins never left off their old Shaivite family Gods such as Ramnath, Nagesh, Ravalnath, &c., nor the Shakta Goddess Mhalsa, &c., even when they became Vaishnavas and for the same reason they could and did pay homage to their former Swami of Kavalay Math and were not in need of a separate Math till some 200 years after Madhva's passing away. In fact, it is the Swami Narayanatirtha, who established a separate Math for the Vaishnavas of the Gowd Saraswat Community.

Accounts vary. It is said that there was already Vishnu worship among the Gowd Saraswat Brahmins before the advent of Madhvacharya, who only changed their "Sidhanta"—system of Philosophy—from the Advaita to his own Dvaita. Madhva himself was worshipping Shiva as the very next God to Shri Krishna, in whose—Shri Krishna's—honour he had built one temple. There are two Shiva temples at Udipi, *viz.*, those of Ananteshwar and Chandra Moulishwar. Madhva was very much devoted to Ananteshwar and used to expound his philosophy and give his daily sermons in that Shaiva temple. And the local tradition insists that Shree Madhvacharya became invisible in a particular spot in the temple by quietly transporting himself body and all to his Heavenly Gods.

The Hindus and especially the Brahmins take their religious dogmas very seriously. It depends on the writer therefore to give any colouring to the subject matter he is interested in. That is how these old Saints have been shown to belong to different and warring schools of worship. The story in connection with the death of Shree Shankaracharya's mother as stated before, is a similar case in point.

Vaishnavism after all did not succeed in uprooting the good old Shaiva and Shakta Gods and Goddesses from the Gowd Saraswat Brahmin Community, who managed to retain their own sturdy faith in them in spite of all the aggressive Vaishnava Saints. Shree Madhva was more concerned, they say, with his particular school of philosophy than with the form of worship, but all the same, these Saraswat Brahmins added some Vaishnava Gods to the fold of their family idols and there the matter has ended. It is said that unlike Chaitanya, who was more concerned with the form of worship, Madhva was concerned with the form of philosophy.

There is one peculiarity among the Gowd Saraswat Brahmins After settling down in Goa, the first thing they did as a religious community highly saturated with Vedantism was to erect their temples. Many of these Gowd Saraswatar have spread themselves all over India. A good many have gone so far south as Travancore, etc. They are to be found in Northern India, where they have settled down in various walks of life for generations and generations together. But thei. Gods in Goa are considered to be the tutelary deities. These family Gods are called Kuladevatas and a Gowd Saraswat Brahmin is bound to come down to Goa, offer his worship and then return back all the distance to the far off place, somewhere in India, where he might be worshipping some local Gods as a temporary measure. In fact these Saraswat Brahmins are very punctilious on the point of visiting their Shrines in Goa, lest their failure to do so, should bring on them the displeasure of their family Gods. This strong affection for their family Gods situate in Goa, carried down from one generation to the other is a strong communal characteristic of these people. Even the great social reformers amongst them are not above quietly sending some money to these temples and getting some ceremonial worship done in the name of one of their near relations.

This attachment to their family Gods in Goa is very strong among the Gowd Saraswatas. They religiously perform the worship of their family Gods—the कुलदेवताराधना—twice every year in the months of Ashwin and Magh and put some cash in a slip box, which every household keeps for this purpose. All that money is forwarded to the temples of their respective family Gods in Goa when the master of the house goes on a pilgrimage there. It is called the कुलदेव यात्रा. Each G. S. Brahmin must perform two such pilgrimages in his life-time.

This community is bound up together through their connection kept up with their family Gods in Goa.

The chief family deities of the Shaivites are :—

1. Shree Mangesh, 2. Shree Shantadurga, 3. Shree Sapta-Kotishwar.

Those belonging to the Vaishnavite section are :—

1. Shree Nagesh, 2. Shree Ramnath, 3. Shree Mahalaxmi, 4. Shree Mahalsa and 5. Shree Laxmi Narasingh. Kamakshâ, Damodar are also among others, well known Vaishnavite Temples. But all the latter deities are Shiva Swarupi. Many of those temples in fact contain Shiva-lingam with the sacred bull in front, practically worshipped as Shiva deities. Their consorts, the Mahalaxmi and Mahalsa are also God Shiva's Shaktis or his consorts. This means that when these people became Vaishṇavites they could not give up the original Gods and Goddesses. Besides these temples devoted to the worship of Vaishnava Gods, contain some sort of a minor idol or idols which are exclusively supposed to be the attendant godlings of the great Lord Shiva. A little image of Parvati and the Shivalinga are to be found within the precincts of the temples. Take for instance the Vaishnavite temple of Shree Ramnath. The chief deity is the idol of Shree Ramnath with idols of Laxmi Narayan, Shantadurga, Vetal Siddhanath, Kamakshâ and Kal Bhairao in attendance.

The idol of Laxmi Narayan was put into this temple, some ten years ago or so by the present Swami of Gokarn Math.

According to Sahyadrikhand and other Puranic traditions, the forefathers of the Gowd Saraswatas brought with them from Tirhut into Goa, the deities of Shree Mangesh, Shree Shantadurga, Shree Sapta Kotishwar, Shree Nagesh, Shree Mahalaxmi, Shree Mahalsa and Kamaksha, when they established themselves there, at the request of Parashuram. Narsingh, Damodar and some others were new additions, after their advent into Goa. All the old Gods were Shaivite or Shakta and this clearly proves that when the people left with them for Goa, they were Shaivites and Shaktas and these were the forms of religion in vogue in Videha, Bengal, &c., in those very early times.

Both Narsimha and Damodar, be it noted, are worshipped in Goa—at Velinga and Zambauli respectively—in Linga forms. Shree Mahalaxmi is that aspect of Durga, spoken of in Saptashati, rather than the ocean-born consort of Vishnu (*vide* Madhyamcharita of Durga Saptashati in Markandeya Puran).

Take another temple of the Vaishnavite Goddess Shree Mahalsa. The chief deity in the centre of the temple is Shree Mahalsa, with Shantadurga, Laxmi Narayan, Ganpati, Gram Purush, Bhagawati, Sonal Bhairao, Kala Bhairao in attendance.

A little description of the idol will be interesting, I think. The image of Shree Mahalasa has four hands. The right upper hand holds a Trishul (Trident), the right lower, a sword. The left upper hand has a drinking bowl, which may be called a Panpatra or perhaps the Surabhajan, alluded to, in the description of some of the forms of Bhagavati, mentioned in the Tantras. The left lower hand holds a severed head. The Goddess stands on a prostrate being whether human or demon, one cannot say. There is an animal like a tiger or a lion, licking the blood from the severed head, held in her hand. There is a necklace on her breast, but it is not clear whether it is made up of skulls. All the Vaishnavas in Goa, South Canara and other places as well belonging to the G. S. Brahmins, look upon this Goddess of Shree Mahalasa, as the Mohini incarnation of Vishnu, which he took after the churning of the Ocean, to kill the demons, who had snatched the nectar pot from the Gods. The Goddess Mahalasa is therefore called by the names of Narayani, Rahu-mathani, Mohini, &c., according to Bhavishya Puran. But looking carefully on the image, its pose, the severed bleeding head and the licking animal at its feet, one is compelled to ponder and cogitate whether one does not see an image of a Shakta Goddess from the Tantras in front of him. The Vaishnavites fully believe it to be an incarnation of Shree Vishnu and let us leave it at that. Scientific research has no business to disturb long established faith in particular sectarian Gods. Similarly Shree Nagesh, a Vaishnavite God in the form of Shiva-linga; is attended on by Kala Bhairao, Ganpati, Ravalnath, etc. Some minor Vaishnavite idols, are said to have been very recently introduced by the present incumbent of the Vaishnavite holy Gadi, Shree Swami Indirakant tirtha of Gokarn Math, who is the religious head of the Vaishnavite Gowd Saraswatas in the North Canara and Goa. He has not however succeeded in dethroning the original Shaiva deities though he has introduced new Vaishnavite deities, alongside.

Even the image of this Shree Nagesh is represented as a pure Lingam at Bandivade, worshipped in a Shaivite form, though most of his worshippers are Vaishnavas.

The following verses which are sung before the Vaishnavite Gods are taken from the official books of the temples and show clearly that the so-called worship of God Vishnu is not an honest one from the genuine Vaishnavite point of view.

त्रिनेत्रा तूं कर्पुर गौरा, त्रिशूळ डमरु दिगंबरा
विभुती भूषण कर भासति हारा, निळकंठ तूं नागेश्वरा
भालचंद्र उमा-वल्लभा भाळें त्रिपुंड्र नमाये-शोभा
जटा मुकूट गंगे[illegible] शोभा, भैरव गण जगमूर्ती उभा ।।

(II)

अगणित लिंगां मानी उत्तम । जगीं प्रसिद्ध रामेश्वर नाम

भक्त जनासी तूं विश्राम । दिव्य स्वरूप तूं परब्रम्ह

त्रिनेत्र तूं कर्पुर गौरा । त्रिशूल डमरु तूं दिगंबरा ॥

etc., etc.

These verses are nothing but praise undiluted of the different attributes of God Shiva. This proves—if any proof is wanted—that the Gowd Saraswat Brahmins, who were originally Smartas and followers of God Shiva, would not and cannot cut themselves off altogether from the worship of God Shiva, even when they were converted to Vaishnavism generations and generations ago. Practically there is no difference either in the form of worship or ceremonies performed in the temples connected with both these sects in Goa. All these temples of the Gowd Saraswat Brahmins are freely open to the members of the community, irrespective of the sect to which, they may belong. Both the sects, the followers of God Shiva and those of God Vishnu, not only visit their own temples but the temples of the other side as well and take an active part in one another's temple ceremonials. Even the priests offer a combined worship to Gods of these two different sects as

श्री मंगेश महालक्ष्मी देवताभ्योनमः

The followers of Shantadurga—a Shakta Goddess—are bound by usage to perform worship at the shrine of Shree Mahalaxmi a Vaishnavite deity when they go on a pilgrimage there. The inter-marriages between these two sects have practically compelled both the different sectarian temples to merge into one another.

The sects of the Smartas as they are styled, which are within the old fold of the Shiva worship are the Shenvis proper, the Shenaipaiki, the Kudaldeshkars (?) the Pednekars, the

Bhala-walkars, the Lotlikars, the Dangis, etc., are other divisions. Those belonging to Vaishnavite cult are called the Sasastikars and the Bardeshkars.

There is a very rich temple called Tirumall Dewaswam in Cochin in the Cochin state. It is a Vaishnavite temple but the Smartas too are the devotees of this temple.

Wonders never cease, they say. As described above, the intolerant Vaishnavism is made to hold a second and inferior place in the Gowd Saraswat Community. Strange to relate, the worship of both the Gods, Shiva and Vishnu, is sometimes performed in the same building as at Chidambaram or as at Shreerang also, if I mistake not. In South Canara and Travancore, the two deities are considered to be of equal greatness. And in some places for instance at Hari-hara in Mysore there are found images representing both these Gods united in one figure. In South Canara there is the famous temple of Shanker-Narayan. But this is a Dravidian Temple, belonging to the Brahmins of that sect.

When the Travancore Kings insisted that Gowd Saraswat Brahmins must go in for the Vaishnavite worship, these people had to agree. But all the same, there was kept concealed in the house a mask either of silver or copper of God Shiva, to whom regular prayers were offered. Even at Belgaum and some of the adjacent places, Gowd Saraswat Vaishnavite Brahmins openly worship these days, the idols of God Shiva.

There is another account which says that when the G. S. Brahmins migrated from Goa into those parts of Cochin and Travancore, they were all Vaishnavas. Further support is given to this by stating that there are no Smarta or Shaiva Temples founded by them, when they settled there. Evidence is forthcoming however that the Gowd Saraswat Brahmins spread themselves all over the Malabar Coast from Goa in the North to Cochin, &c.,

in the South. In fact, if my memory serves me right, there were three migrations from Trihotrapur in Videha (Northern Behar) and other places in Northern India at different times. There is besides a Shaiva temple at Manjeshwar, South Canara. This Temple of Shree Ananteshwar at Manjeshwar belongs to all the G. S. Brahmins residing all along the West Coast. There is a Linga of Ananteshwar and images of Nrisimha and Naga (serpent). These serpent images go also by the name of Subrahmanya, Skanda or Kartikeya. The local car festival comes off every year on Champa-Shasti day, which is however better known there as the Skanda-Shashti day. This falls on the 6th day of the bright half of the month Margashirsha. This Ananteshwar Temple is the most important one on the Malabar Coast. It is supposed to be the only "Kuldeva" *i.e.* the family or tutelary temple of the Gowd Saraswatas, living so far south as Cochin, Travancore, &c. This temple was built long before the 8th century A.D. Mr. M. Govind Pai considers that this temple must have belonged originally to the Dravidian Brahmins. If that be so, it is a mystery how it came under the full and absolute control of the G. S. Brahmins. The form of worship is pure and simple Vaishnavite. There are five Lingas in all but only one at the back is worshipped by a Vaishnava Brahmin in a Quasi-Shaiva form. This Linga is called Mahadev. The prime Linga of Anant in the forefront, is worshipped as the "Serpent King" incarnation of Vishnu and the "endlessness" form of Shiva, combined in one. There is a serpent's hole in the Sanctum Sanctorium, which is called Vasuki-mandir, and is also worshipped.

On the Madras side, even interdining is not allowed between these two sects but among the Gowd Saraswatas not only they freely dine with each other but they have of late gone in for inter-marriages as well, the prohibition of marriage between the same Gotra and Pravara as well as Sapindas being carefully observed.

When asked why should a Smarta go to the temple of a Vaishnavite, the answer is, Oh they are all one. The same Shakti, the same God-like essence is in them all. We visit our own idols first and we are in duty bound to visit other temples afterwards, irrespective of whether they are Vaishnavites or Shaivites. From the nature of Kuladevatas or the tutelary deities worshiped by these Brahmins and looking to the fact that they were in the olden times the priests carefully brought up in Vedic rituals, it is no wonder to see that the later cults of either Gods, Shiva and Vishnu, did not produce that vibration in their minds, as they did in the comparatively uncultured people of later generations. That is why the philosophical doctrines inculcated in the Shrutis and the tonets in the Smritis had a penetrating influence on their minds so much so that they have not been able to shake that off, after centuries and centuries of idol worship. The cult of Shree Shankaracharya being closely connected with the Vedic philosophy superimposed with the worship of God Shiva, has found favour with these people.

The wave of Vaishnavism was not an ordinary placid affair. It broke out in tempestuous currents devouring everything that came in its way. It had a peculiar fascination for the backward Hindu communities. But this fascination, this popularity, this onward rush of pure Bhakti might have shaken the citadel of Shaivism a good deal but all that never succeeded in touching the inner religious consciousness of these Gowd Saraswat Brahmins. They simply bowed down their heads to the wave and allowed it to pass on but after the first onset was over they have come back to the old, old religion of theirs.

Perhaps it may be due to the fact that the Gowd Saraswatas were originally the followers of Bhagawat sect in ages past which made no distinction between Vishnu and Shiva.

The ever popular deity the Vithoba of Pandharpur, the God Narasingh the family God of Vijayanagar dynasty, Shree Venkatramana of Tirupati, a deity popular with the Vaishnavites are some other Gods that are worshipped to a more or less extent by all the Gowd Saraswatas. But no family has denounced or ceased to take an active part or some personal interest in their Kula-devatas which are in Goa. This personal interest may lie dormant for some years and years but all the same, sooner or later something gets awakened in the Gowd Saraswat soul and drives him back to Goa, willy nilly, to prostrate himself before the tutelary deities originally brought from Tirhut.

THE KONKANI FOLK-LORE TALES.

By Rao Saheb Dr. V. P. Chavan, L. M. & S.

THE STORY OF THE JAMBOO FRUIT.

Once upon a time, in a certain state, there lived a Rajah who had a charming daughter. There was also another Rajah in the same territory, the father of a handsome prince. Both the young prince and the pretty princess used to attend the same school. On their way to the Pâtshala, they used to indulge in all sorts of mischievous pranks. On the road to the school, there was a Jamboo tree, loaded with good and luscious fruit. The school children were very fond of climbing the tree and enjoying the fruit. The prince as well as the princess were in no way backward in following their school mates high up the tree. But there was one rule and it was strictly observed. When the princess was the first to arrive at the tree, it was she who should go up the tree and pluck the fruit, which should be gathered together by the prince from the ground below the tree. If the prince came in first, he had to throw down the fruit, which was collected by the princess standing on the ground.

Well, it so happened once that the princess was the first to arrive at the tree when returning from the school. She got up the tree. The prince, who arrived late, had to stand at the foot of the tree. The princess asked the prince what sort of fruit he would like to have. Do you want the hot or the cold fruit ? It was a puzzle and the prince could not understand what she meant by hot and cold fruit. The fruit that was on the tree was of the same sort. Some was ripe, some was green. But nothing hot nor cold was to be found on that tree. The prince could not solve the riddle. Come on, said the princess "don't you be standing there like a fool." The prince got annoyed and said, drop both the sorts of fruit, hot and cold. Hurry up.

The princess plucked some fruit, rubbed it nicely between her palms and threw it down. "This is the hot variety," she said. "Go on. Eat it up." The prince could not eat the fruit as it was covered with sand without blowing it away. Then some fruit was thrown down, fresh from the stem without any rubbing. That was cold fruit, which the prince swallowed without wiping or blowing on it.

The school children dispersed as the game was over. But the prince—still puzzled—would not let the princess go home, without her giving him a full explanation of the incident. What was the significance of the words—hot and cold, he asked. The princess laughed at his stupidity and told the prince that she had taken him for a man with some brains. Well, here is the explanation, you dullard, she said. Two sorts of fruit were dropped down. The first *sort* the hot one, which I had rubbed together in my palms, could not be enjoyed by you, without blowing away the sand which would have soiled your mouth. Now put on your cap of wisdom and let us hear when do you blow at a thing before eating ? When it is hot, is it not so ? The second sort which you swallowed, immediately after picking it up, was the cold variety because you could put it into your mouth without blowing on it. Now, I hope, the princess cried, you understand the significance of the words—hot and cold!

The prince saw red. His face got flushed at being made a fool by the clever princess. He looked at her. The sparkling eyes, the pouting lips and the mischievous look, all captivated the prince. Princess! said he I am going to marry you. I am determined to do so simply to get down your cleverness, a peg or two. Immediately after marriage I am going to confine you in a fortress deep down in the forest, where you will not be able to see anybody except your own maid-servants. That will teach you a lesson. Alone and solitary, you will have plenty of time to grow "hot and cold" as the fancy seizes you.

"Agreed"! said the Princess, who was considerably ruffled. But on one condition! Mind! you will have to come and acknowledge me as your wedded wife and treat me with the respect due to me as such, when you are slapped on your face by your own son born out of our wedlock, with your own shoes. The prince took up the challenge, as there was clearly no possibility of their ever being together.

The prince and the princess took leave of each other and went to their respective places. Their respective parents had already put in their heads together about the union of the two families. And this ripple in the youngsters' amiable relations made them hurry up the marriage. It was celebrated with all the eclat befitting such an auspicious occasion and the princess, in course of time, came to live in the palace of the prince.

But the prince had not forgotten his vow nor the ridicule to which he was subjected by the princess at the Jamboo tree. He had quietly managed to have a fortress ready, deep in the jungles, where he took his wife and her maids and locked them in. The fortress was well supplied with stores. It was also well guarded. There was no marital kiss.

The prince used to go and visit his wife, now and then, just to satisfy himself that his wife, the princess, had no communication whatsoever with the outside world. Several years passed. On account of the cruelty practised on his first and only wife, the prince could not get married again. He was shunned and avoided by the then society. He organised a circus and went all over the country to detract his attention. In course of time, the circus came into a town, close to the fortress. The latter was well looked after, no doubt, but, one way or other, all outside news was conveyed to the inmates of the prison.

The princess came to know of the advent of her husband in the guise of a circus proprietor. She put on a cap of wisdom and considered the ways and means to join her husband. The princess had a Moongoos given to her by her mother, of which she was fond. She got the Moongoos to burrow a hole through the fortress walls. Seeing that the princess made no effort, whatever, for a good many years, to escape, the discipline had become somewhat lax. The princess saw her way out. She disguised herself thoroughly and went to the circus and offered her services as an acrobat. Her well-developed figure, her charm, her horseman-ship all these made her to be engaged on the spot. The prince, under whose superintendence she worked, fell under her smiles. Do the clouds cover up the beauty of the full Moon? Her poor dress, her menial position could not conceal the graceful beauty of her form, nor did the hearts surrounding her, remain unaffected by her glances. The dis-consolate prince was the most smitten. These glances rendered him thoroughly uncomfortable and unsettled, harassing his imagination, vexing his conscience and confusing his principles and prejudices in harsh and hopeless discord.

He offered to marry her. "I am already married," the Princess replied but she had no objection to live in his society, provided his signet ring was given to her as a present. After passing sometime in his company, the princess quietly stole back to her prison, where, in course of time, she gave birth to a son.

The prince lost his reason in fact, at the disappearance of his *in amorata*. His condition was pitiable. For him the joy and wonder of youth were over. He was pretty sure that the circus lady had a sincere love for him. The prince had taken to a wandering life to forget his troubles. The lady had appeared to the prince as a drop of water does to the long expectant and thirsty Châtak bird. The prince went away with his circus to countries far away to drown his sorrow in hard work and it was some four years before he returned to his native place.

He went to the fortress to see how his wife was going on. The princess kept her son concealed when the prince came there. After his meals, the prince sat outside in the verandah. She took the shoes of her husband, which were kept outside, went to her son, and asked him to use those shoes on the face of her husband. The little urchin took the whole thing as a joke and gave a beating to the prince with the shoes. The prince wondered how a male child came into the fortress, caught hold of him and began to ill-use him. Beating a man with a shoe is considered the greatest affront in Indian Society. The princess came running and it came out that the child was her son. The prince's wrath knew no bounds. Calling all sorts of names to his wife for her so-called un-faithfulness to her marriage vows, he made up his mind to have her beheaded.

The princess proud in the glory of her innocence, put before the prince the signet ring and informed him that she was the lady who had joined his circus as an acrobat some four years back. She could easily convince him on that point. The prince had to bow his head in shame. But all the same, he felt proud of his wife, whose cleverness and intellect had surmounted all difficulties and who had managed to fulfill her vow. The light of an absolute adoration shone in his eyes when he embraced them both. There was a grand procession to his palace and they lived ever happily to the end of their days.

THE KONKANI FOLK-LORE TALES.
THE CUPIDITY OF A BRAHMIN.

There used to live in a certain village a very poor Brahmin with his wife and children. He managed to exist by begging from door to door. After a time the villagers got tired of supporting the Brahmin and his increasing family and gave him to understand that he had better move to some other part of the country. On an auspicious day, the Brahmin started with his family to parts un-known. He came into a forest. By the time they had reached the middle part of it, they found that the Sun had set and everything was wrapt up in gloom and darkness. The children were hungry and exhausted. The Brahmin and his wife were also in a similar predicament. They could hardly move their limbs. The jungle contained a good many briers and some of these got into their soles and feet. What with pain and utter weariness, they all began to bewail their fate. Mid-night approached and there was black pitchy darkness everywhere. There were cries of wild animals, the howling of jackals and the hooting of owls. All this made the night doubly dreadful. The people continued weeping, wailing and praying. They called on their Gods to relieve them of their misery. Was there any chance of their prayers being heard? Hardly any. But they were good Brahmins. In the meanwhile, it so happened that the God Shiva with his consort the Goddess Parvati, was out taking a stroll in the forest. It was Parvati whose heart yearned to relieve the distress of the Brahmin. They disclosed themselves to the Brahmin and his wife and asked them the cause of their bewailing their fate. The Brahmin narrated his life's story, concealing nothing. God Shiva took pity on them and presented them with three cocoanuts informing them that any one of them should concentrate on any one wish and break open the cocoanut and that wish would be fulfilled. With a parting blessing, the Gods had vanished.

The Brahmin took one of the nuts and prayed " Let our pain, hunger and thirst vanish, and let us be taken to the village where we lived." Immediately they found themselves back in the village. Then the Brahmin, concentrating on his desire to have a good many fields and land, broke open nut number two. He became a rich man.. Wishing for a mansion etc. the third nut shared the fate of the first two and the Brahmin became the owner of a splendid building. All this meant that the poverty stricken Brahmin became the Kuber—a wealthy man of the village.

The news of the sudden accession to wealth, spread like wild-fire in the neighbouring villages. People from outlying villages came in their tens and hundreds to know, how the Brahmin had managed to become wealthy so easily and quickly.

He told them all that had happened when he got into the forest, after leaving the village, how darkness overtook them, how thorns found resting places in their feet, how they cried and prayed and how the Gods appeared and blessed them and gave them the Cocoanuts etc. The villagers were glad to see the Brahmin family in affluence and went their different ways. But there was one Brahmin avaricious and crafty, who wanted to become as rich as the Brahmin.

So one day the crafty Brahmin sold all what he had, including his house etc. and deposited the money with a local Sowcar. He took his wife and children and went in the evening to the same forest where the original Brahmin had met the Gods. As they, the Brahmins, were well shod, no thorns entered their feet. But the Brahmin's wife had taken some nails with her, which she thrust into the soles of her husband and her children as well. The children had a very exhausting day already and the putting in of the nails into their feet, made them bawl out.

To them also came the God Shiva and his consort the Goddess Parvati.

Before the Gods could ask any questions, the Brahmin's wife called out to Shiva. Oh! Lord! We are very poor people. Give us those cocoanuts which you gave to the other Brahmin a few days back. God Shiva understood their character very well but out of pure greatness of his heart, he gave them three cocoanuts and departed.

But the avaricious Brahmin forgot one thing. He was covetous. His wife was much more so. His children well they were the product—a sort of square root of these two. It never entered into their heads to give up the Jam pot in order to appreciate clean bread and butter. Every body wanted to have his own wish fulfilled by breaking open a cocoanut. Besides the cocoanuts contained the milk as they were fresh ones. The thirsty children were clamorous. One of them took up a cocoanut and would not listen to any reason. When the mother found that the child was going to break open the cocoanut without expressing a definite wish, she got excited and uttered the words " Your mother's head." What she wanted to convey was—don't break open the nut. If you do, it will be as bad as breaking open your mother's head. But the result was awful. The child broke open the cocoanut and his mother concentrated on the wish " your mother's head." The process was complete. The poor lady was covered from top to bottom with all sorts of heads. There were numbers of them. There were heads growing from the feet and the legs and the shoulders and the arms, and the back and the front. In fact there was not a single space on her body which did not produce a head big or small. The effect was frightening and hideous. All the heads looked piteously at the Brahmin and began to jabber—Oh! Save me, my lord and husband from these heads. The Brahmin had lost his wits. He caught hold of a cocoanut and dashed it on the ground saying let all the heads go away. Well, the wish was fulfilled. All the heads disappeared including the original one too, of the Brahmin lady. The headless trunk began to dance in front of her husband. The sight was awful. Something had to be done and that too in a hurry. Snatching the remaining cocoanut he prayed for the return of the original head. It came back.

But all the three nuts were done away with and the Brahmin and his family were, where they were before. No—they were in a worse condition in fact. They began to cry and wail again. They did so with a vehemence and enthusiasm unknown before. There were real genuine tears this time. No nails were required to draw those tears out. They waited and waited but waited in vain for the Gods to appear but none appeared. The Saints and the angels who are rightly supposed to look after the holy Brahmin did not have even a twist of a thought for them.

Morning broke. Each hour made their condition uglier and hungrier and more hopeless and they had to return to their village, dejected and starving. But their troubles were not over.

To those who are down, the world is a harsh, hard, cold and a cross sort of a place. The Sowcar with whom they had deposited the sale-proceeds of their property, had made himself scarce. Higher rate of interest had made the avaricious Brahmin, place his money with him. The Brahmin had mixed his life's colours and the final colour in his existence was the dirty black one— that of his begging bowl which he had to carry from door to door to support himself.

THE KONKANI FOLK-LORE TALES.

THE BRAN MAID.

In a certain part of the country, not far off from Mangalore, there lived a rich Zemindar who had seven daughters and as many sons. One day he called his daughters together and asked them, at whose expense they were going to enjoy the sweets of life ? "May Bhagwan Krishna give you long life, Oh ! father !" The eldest six replied. "We are very happy and comfortable under you. Here the life is following smooth." Their wheedling tongues carried joy to the old man's heart. Turning to the youngest, the father invited her to give her opinion. You will have to support me, father, till I am twelve, the age when I expect to get married. After that I shall have to depend on my own fortune and kismet for my maintenance. This straight-forward answer ruffled the temper of the old man. This youngest daughter was the prettiest of the whole lot. Her charming manners, her graceful behaviour and her cleverness had made her the Beau Ideal in the family. Her elder sisters were naturally jealous of her and took full advantage to fan the flame of the father's anger. He lost his temper. Now that you are so wise as to think of your marriage and independence, the best thing for you would be, you naughty girl, to have a taste of that independence even from now. Get away from my sight.

A small hut was built for her and she was put there. The mother could not help feeling for her and she managed to get permission from her husband, to supply the little child with some bran at least. That is how, the girl came to be known in the country as the bran maid.

Her brothers were merchants trading with far off countries. Starting on a voyage they took a fancy to ask their sisters, what the latter would like as presents from foreign countries. Some wanted gold Sarees, others jewellery and so on. The poor neglected bran maid was also asked what sort of a present she would like to have. The starved little thing thought that they were making fun of her. She told them therefore to bring her "the life sustaining-substance" meaning thereby that they would bring some substantial sort of food for her.

They prospered on their voyage. It was time for them to return. The brothers bought the various articles asked by their sisters but they clean forgot all about the life sustaining substance, treating it as a joke. They weighed anchor. But the ship would not be moved. They tried various means to sail the ship but it was a fixture. One of the brothers then remembered about the present to his youngest sister—the bran maid. As the ship could not be moved, they had perforce to get down. They inquired at the various places for the substance but they could not come across any. At the last moment however, a merchant who was really a prince, listened to their tale of the strange substance and the history of the bran maid. He promised to supply them with the life sustaining substance if they would wait some time. The prince hurried to his quarters. He filled a small box with different sorts of jewellery, added to it a nice Saree and also a magical mirror. The box was then thickly covered up with clay and small stones, which made it look like a ball of mud and stones and handed it over to the brothers for the small price of Rs. 500.

There was no difficulty this time for the ship to sail. They made a quick journey home and the mud ball was handed in due course to the bran maid. She took it as a huge joke and placed it in front of her hut to be used as a stepping stone.

Some years passed and our bran maid entered into her womanhood. Her beauty, her sympathy with the poor neighbours of hers, her hard life, all these had developed a peculiar fascinating charm in her. The rains had gradually washed off the clayey covering in course of years, exposing the box concealed inside. One day the bran girl stepped on the box, which was broke open. She took it inside the hut and removed the contents. No sooner that was done, her hut got changed into a beautiful place, seven storeyed high. She found herself sitting in a splendid room on the topmost storey. The place was surrounded by seven walls each wall being guarded by armed sentries. She was filled with wonder. She put on the Saree and the ornaments. Woman's curiosity made her look into the mirror to see how she looked and lo! the prince appeared—the very prince who had sent her that box with her brothers. The branmaid's cup of happiness was complete. The glorious sunshine of youth and love lay like a quickening fire on their hearts.

Life is made ugly, vicious and detestable on account of the pestilential temperament known as jealousy. The sisters were furious. They could not see the bran maid happy with the newly awakened light of love in her eyes. They tried her with poisoned sweets. But the bran maid gave them to her dogs and cats, only to find them dead, time after time. The jealous sisters coaxed her into telling them how the prince managed to see her? A particular window was shown through which the prince used to fly to his lady *inamorata*. The sisters quietly arranged to place a sharp sword in the window and departed home. As usual, the bran maid looked into the magic mirror but the prince came not. She looked again into it but still there was no prince. She got alarmed and went to the window to wait for him, only to find the head of the prince lying there, all bloody, separated from the body. There was no trace of the body whatsoever. Her grief knew no bounds. Where could she go for her consolation and sympathy! Poor and neglected as she was, her prayers to Heaven were as simple and as straight as those of a little child. Life became absolutely impregnated with wretchedness.

The next morning she put the head into a box and disguised herself as a beggar and took to the road. What has become of the prince's body—was the question agitating her mind. In course of time she came to the outskirts of a big town and she laid herself to sleep under a big pipal tree.

The prince had taught her not only the language of love but that of birds as well. There were a good many glow worms there. What about this strange disappearance of the head of our prince, one of them asked of his companion. It is not to be found anywhere. The body is alive. There is life in it. What is this mystery ? There is nothing mysterious in this, said the other glow worm. The prince fell in love with a beauteous maid and used to visit her. Her sisters got jealous and managed to have his head cut off. Where is that head please ? Look at the maid crying her eyes out here, below our tree. She has got the head and she is in search of the body of her prince. But what would be the use of finding out the body with the head off it ? There you are mistaken, said the glow worm. If the maid collects a few pounds of our castings and mixes it up thoroughly with 36 gallons of milk and fixes the head carefully on the trunk with the help of this paste, the prince will get up as sound as a bell. A question of ten minutes only.

The bran maid understood the whole thing clearly. She quickly collected the castings of the glow worm and waited anxiously for the day to break. Love is eternal and it is only pain and grief and sin that can come to an end. The turmoil produced in her heart by the joy that she had come to the end of her quest and she was going to restore her beloved to his full bodily vigour—all these happy and joyous thoughts made the maid look the very essence of a sun-beam. Morning broke. With a palpitating heart and a shaking hand, she collected the castings of the worms and started to the place where the body was kept.

But who would allow a beggar woman clothed in rags to enter the palace and far less to approach the body of the prince surrounded by specialists from all parts of the world. The king was there. The Queen too was there, each supporting the other in their over-powering grief. But the beggar maid was firm. She would not be moved from the palace doors. Here I have come to restore the prince to his life and here I stay till my mission is fulfilled. Her resolute mien, her eyes flashing with the light of determination, her persistence, her woe-begone expression made the court attendants carry the news to the king. Let her have a chance, said the king who had given up all hopes of restoring the prince to life. But one thing I demand, said the maid as the price of my success. I must have the signet ring which the prince is wearing on his finger. Nothing more, nothing less. The king agreed and the body was taken to a room. The maid arranged the head very carefully and smeared the whole part with the paste prepared according to the glow worm's directions. Ten minutes passed. The prince came to life as if awakened from sleep and stretched his legs. He saw the maid clothed in rags and asked his attendants to remove her from his presence. Certainly he did not recognise her. The king explained to him what had happened and asked him to present the maid with his ring. The prince would not part with it. "It is meant for the lady I am going to marry and for no one else," said he. Let the beggar maid have gold, jewels and even a portion of the kingdom but the ring she would not have. The maid too was equally firm. She held the king to his promise and threatened him that her magic would be undone and the head might fly away again. Then and then only, the prince sorrowfully parted with his ring.

The bran-maid, let us give her original name—returned to her palace and looked into the magic mirror one evening invoking her prince to come to her. Ah ! The joy of joys ! The beloved, the long-lost prince was there, telling her all sorts of love absurdities. Love is the water of Life. It was fascinating. Well, the prince commenced to tell her all that had happened to him and the maid sat mute. The ring—he did not like to part with it, but that physician woman insisted on having it and so it was lost. The bran maid quietly put her hand before the prince with the ring shining on it. The prince recognised it and there were more explanations. The love that had gone through the fiery ordeal, made both the hearts unite in a firm embrace. And charity which springs out of perfect Love, made them forget the treachery and venom of the sisters. The marriage took place with all the pomp and splendour befitting the occasion and it is needless to say that both the prince and his wife had but one hope, one desire, one course of life and one service of God in common with one another.

THE KONKANI FOLKLORE TALES.

THE CRUEL STEP MOTHER.

Once upon a time there lived a Brahmin who had an only daughter. His wife was a very good woman and both the parents loved their daughter very dearly. Just close to them, there lived an old woman of the same community.

The woman was in straitened circumstances and she was asked to look after the Brahmin girl, dress her hair and send her back when the playtime was over. The girl who was hardly four or five years old, took a natural liking for her nurse. Now the old woman had a daughter of her own and she was growing fast. Hindu Shastras enjoin that girls must be married before they attain puberty. The old woman was a wicked magician. She wanted to marry her daughter to the Brahmin but that was not possible during the lifetime of the wife. So she began to cast her magical charms on the little Brahmin girl and poison her mind against her own mother. She said to the little girl, "I take so much care of you, dress you properly, give you a nice bath that I have come to love you, as my own child. My daughter too loves you. While your cruel hearted mother scolds you if you are late, does not allow you to eat sweets as much as you would like to have and punishes you in season and out of season. What is the use of having such a mother? We both slave all the day looking after you and we have been taking every possible care of you." Day by day the same poison was instilled into the baby's mind and she began to look on her mother as a sort of demon. The wicked woman went a step further. She succeeded in persuading the little child to plant an open knife just near where the ladder was placed to go up to the attic. The wife of the Brahmin was in the habit of keeping sweet stuff high up in the attic with a view to prevent her daughter from eating too much. The wicked woman had turned the little child's mind like wax and had asked her to remove the ladder when her mother was trying to climb down. The poor-poor child had no idea of what she was doing and shoved aside the ladder when the mother was coming down, with the result that the poor lady fell down on the open knife and breathed her last. The funeral rites were performed in the usual manner and the Brahmin was left to mourn the loss of his wife. But from that moment, happiness fled from that house.

The wicked woman now had her chance. She began to minister to the wants of the lone Brahmin. Her daughter too took an interest in the household affairs. The little orphan was made much off. She was made to call the wicked woman's daughter by the name of mother. Sometimes, the household work was purposely neglected and the father and his small daughter had to look after themselves. The little girl was again taken in hand. Oh! My beloved darling, why does not your father marry my daughter? She is full grown and I shall have to get her married soon. And when she is married, I go with her to pass the few days' that are left to me. In that case, there will not be anybody here to look after you and your good father. The Brahmin who was considerably shaken at the death of his wife and who was a simple straightforward man, fell into the snare and married the wicked woman's daughter.

A few weeks passed away and both the old lady as well as the new step-mother began to exert their authority against the poor waif. The latter became the drudge of the house. The step mother used to take her ease and roll about, making the little step daughter work her bones off. There was not much food given to her and what little she got, was of the coarse variety. Misery ripened her intelligence and she knew that she was made a tool of, by these wicked women. Her prayers to her dead mother were incessant. All the drudgery she had to undergo, all the semi-starvation she had to suffer, did not break her spirit. Her full faith in her idols, her remembrance of her mother's sweet face, put new courage in her soul. "Bless me" Oh! my mother and give me strength to bear up with the tribulations. One night her mother approached her in her dream, blessed her and assured her that sooner or later her troubles would be over. Even the gold had to pass through the fire to be worthy of being turned into ornaments which even a Queen would be proud to wear round her neck. But one thing, my child, you must be careful of. Do all the work your stepmother asks you to do. But beware of eating anything that she may place before you. If you feel hungry, go to the south wall of our house and ask for Chappaties and shut your eyes and the Chappaties will be placed before you. If you want butter, go to the pond and stir the water with your fingers and you may find butter there. Ask the cows for some milk. The cocoanut tree will supply you with the nuts. The dream was vivid and it left a tranquillity and a calm peace in the poor girl's heart, unknown there before. The walls gave her the Chappaties, the pond the butter, the cows the milk. And she was happy in her own small way.

In the meanwhile, the step mother had a daughter who was growing up. When she was 4 or 5 years old, the baby used to accompany the Brahmin girl. This little cousin came to know how her cousin the Brahmin girl used to get her food. Being of obstinate nature she wanted to get the food herself. So the step-mother's daughter asked the wall to serve her with Chappaties.

But instead, a stone came rushing and broke one of her legs. She did manage to crawl to the pond, which was near by and stirred the water asking for butter. But a fish quietly took her thumb off. The cocoanut threw a nut on her head when she begged for one. Thinking that the cow would at least supply her with milk, she went to the animal and got a good kick on one of her eyes. The Brahmin girl took her cousin in that state to her mother. When the latter saw her child's condition, she pommelled severely her step-daughter and locked her up in a room. How to get rid of her, became the burning question with her.

There was a powerful King in a neighbouring town. It seems that he had fallen under a curse of a Holy Rishi, who had turned the King's poor son into an alligator, who had to be fed daily with a virgin girl. As the girls became scarcer, the Rajah's servants began to score the country from one end to the other, buying girls at the rate of one thousand rupees each. One of those servants came to the house of this step-mother, who found a golden opportunity of not only getting rid of her step-daughter but getting good money as well. She quietly pocketed the money, handing over the girl to her terrible fate without the least pity or mercy.

The Brahmin-girl was confined in a cage and there she came to know that she was to be thrown into the pond to the alligator. She called on her mother to receive her. She prayed to her gods to take her unto them as she was tired of life. Kicked and starved, death was preferable to the existence she hed carried. Mother! Oh! Mother darling, keep me with you ever long now. I am not afraid of the alligator. He is simply the means—a sort of horse that will convey me quickly to you, Oh! Mother mine! The Lord Parameshwar and his divine Goddess Parvati heard the wailing of the poor girl. They came down to her and got the whole story of her life from her. Devi Parvati pitied the poor waif. She blessed her and gave her some "Akshata"—rice grains—flowers and a cane and told her to throw some of the rice grains and flowers on the alligator when he came to devour her. Give him a cut also with the cane. He will turn back and then will come again rushing at you. Do the whole process again. The third time he comes at you, throw all the rice and flowers on his head and let him have five cuts with the cane on the head. This will destroy the magic of the holy Brahmin and the alligator will be turned into a handsome prince, whom you will marry.

The girl was thrown into the pit, the next day. But she was bold enough to do all the things desired by the Gods and succeeded in turning the beast into a handsome prince. There were great rejoicings in the country and the Prince could not but love and marry the Brahmin-girl.

But it seems that the girl had to undergo some more trials before she was completely purified of her share of putting an end to her own mother's life. The step-mother came to know that the Brahmin girl had become a princess by marriage and she set her brain working again to destroy her. Some time passed and the princess was now in the family way. It is a custom with the Hindoos that the first confinement must take place at her mother's place. The step-mother insisted that her daughter must come to her for her confinement. She was all smiles. She stood on her rights as the mother who had brought up that orphan girl after the death of her mother and as one belonging to a poor but noble family, she insisted that nobody, be he a prince or a common man should dare to come in her way of getting her daughter to her father's place for her first delivery. She succeeded in getting the princess back to her home.

On an auspicious day, the princess gave birth to a son. The villagers made grand preparations to celebrate the event. The Prince hurried down. On the tenth day after delivery—this side of Konkan we give the bath on the eleventh day—the usual oil bath was given to the lady. The step-mother was very busy in getting ready hot water, the various perfumed oils, and the various fragrant spices to be used as dusting powders. But the step-mother had not lost the least bit of her venom against the poor princess. She got a deep pit dug up and some open knives were placed therein. The pit was covered up with rotten planks. The Princess was placed on them and very hot water was poured over her head. She could not bear that and she struggled naturally. The planks gave way throwing the princess down on the open knives where she breathed her last as her own mother had done some years ago. The cries of the princess could not be heard outside, where the Prince her husband and other notabilities were sitting, on account of the beating of tom-tom.

Having fully expiated her sin, the princess joined her mother in Swargalok (heaven) where the celestial nymphs lived.

The step-mother made all hurry to put the special dress on her own daughter and passed her off as the Princess. Things went on smoothly for some time. The prince had his doubts about his wife but he attributed all those to a change in her disposition on account of the confinement and the trouble of the baby, whose cries could not be stopped.

There is a custom with us that the wife should present her husband with a small packet—called *Vida*—made up of betel leaves, betel-nut and spices etc. and keep a supply of these materials by the bed side of her husband. But the prince always found his silver-pot empty, which was regularly filled up at bed time. He asked his wife what became of all those betel-leaves and other chewing materials?

The supposed wife pleaded ignorance and brought to the notice of the Prince another strange incident. "Some ghosts in the shape of celestial nymphs," said she, "come every night to my room, take up the baby, put him to the breast, play with him and then put him to bed and go away."

But before they disappear, they spit at me the red saliva which is formed in the mouth after chewing the pan supari.

"What a strange story you tell me," exclaimed the prince ! The prince did not go to sleep that night but kept himself awake in his bed watching and watching what would happen. Midnight passed. Nothing happened. He waited anxiously. After some time he heard musical jingling of silver anklets. There was a sensation of a cool breeze passing over him, loaded with a pleasing scent. He found some nymphs, quietly helping themselves to betel leaves etc. The prince kept quiet and awaited further developments. The ladies then went into the room where the baby was kept. One of them took it up and put it to the breast. The other nymphs began to dance round it. Tickling the baby's feet, kissing it, putting flowers on its head and other gambols took up their time. The step-mother's daughter the false wife—was thoroughly frightened. The nymphs began to spit the betel nut juice on the wife's person. She fainted. The baby was then put to sleep again and the nymphs began to walk away. The prince who was watching all their play, stepped forth and caught hold of the lady who had suckled the baby and asked her the reason why she was so kind to his child. The lady hung down her head and kept quiet. Her companions however, chided the prince for not recognising his own true wife and explained to him all the incidents that led to the murder. The prince was awe-struck. His rage caused him to tremble and quake. But the ladies quieted him and made him promise to keep quiet a few weeks more. The " Anna-prashan " or Ushtavan day is fast approaching and many a learned Shastri and Pundit would be attending the ceremony and you better leave the punishment to them. When a baby gets a tooth or two, the putting in, of some food-boiled rice etc. into his mouth is called the Anna-prashan ceremony. We would be there too, Oh ! Prince, with your wife. So keep your soul in patience and go out on a pilgrimage till then. The day arrived. The prince was there too. Holy Brahmins were there. A good many Shastris and Nyayis were there too. The Apsarâs were present also. The prince called in the learned men into the room, where his false wife was present and put his case before them. The guilty woman acknowledged her share in the murder of the real princess but the story of her grand mother's wickedness as well as that of her mother also came out. The pundits decided that these three generations of women were nothing but personification of Evil. The grand-mother is dead. The mother and this her daughter—the false wife are adjudged guilty. As a Brahmin male or female cannot be decapitated, we sentence this girl as well as her mother. The false wife is to be tied hand and foot and should be placed in the basket kept in a privy. And we assure you that the Fates would overtake her mother also.

The step-mother did not know of what had happened to her daughter. She was giving herself grand airs that her dastardly plot had succeeded. And that her own daughter would reign as a queen in course of time. She was busy with her preparations of the grand feast. The real princess, the real wife quietly took her place by the side of her husband, when the Annaprashan ceremony was performed. The next morning when the step-mother went to answer the call of nature, she found her daughter there in the basket covered with filth, on the point of death. The daughter abused her mother and told her plainly that all her scheming, all her wickedness had resulted in this sort of abominable death. The step-mother got a shock and fell down dead by the side of her dead daughter.

The Konkani proverb says "Bin takit bhât" *i.e.*, as is the seed, so is the paddy. Nothing but evil comes out of evil. The prince returned to his palace with his wife and his darling baby. And they lived ever happily afterwards.

THE KONKANI FOLK LORE TALES.

THE TALE OF THE WAX-DOLL AND THE COW-DUNG DOLL.

Once upon a time, a wax doll and a cowdung doll went on a pilgrimage to the sea. The tide was coming in and the two companions stood on the shore close to the sea, gazing with wondrous eyes at the beauty of the waves and the noise and the foam which they produced. A wave larger than the rest, came dashing along and covered up both the dolls and retreated. The cow-dung doll was dissolved by the action of the water. The grief of the wax doll knew no bounds. It stood there, planting its feet firmly on the ground and began to ask of the sea to restore its friend, the cow-dung doll back to her. Its cries became insistence. But the sea could not bring the cow dung doll to life again and it was arranged that the wax doll should be given a cot in exchange, that was floating in the sea just close by. The wax doll put the cot on its head and began to travel to some other holy shrine. It came to a fence and feeling tired, placed the cot by the fence and went out for a bath. By the time it returned, the cot had disappeared. The doll got excited and turned on the fence threatening it with all sorts of dire consequences, unless the cot was returned. The fence could not do that but humbly requested the doll to take away any two poles supple and strong and forgive it. The doll shouldered the two poles and came in course of time to a cottage, where an old woman was engaged in baking Chapatties. It kept the poles near the woman's door and went out for a wash. After its return, it was found that the old woman had quietly used those poles for lighting her kitchen-fire. The wax-doll managed to get two good Chapatties, out of the old woman and walked proudly away. It was very careful of those Chapatties and found out a house—a dilapidated building where no human being was likely to come and kept those Chapatties inside and went out for a sniff of fresh breeze but the wax-doll had forgotten about the rats, that were there, which made a clean sweep of the Chapatties in no time. The doll returned and had a good tussle with the house before the latter agreed to part with a drum that was lying hanging in a corner.

Tying the drum around its neck, the doll began to beat it before a Rajah's palace and sing a ditty as follows :—

"A cot I got for the cow-dung doll,

"And exchanged it with the fence for poles.

"The old woman gave me Chapatties two
"For the poles. What else could I do?
"The Chapatties I kept in a ruined house
"To feed only the dog, the cat and the mouse.
"I cried and cried and got this drum
"Happy, happy I am! Dum, dum, dum!!!

THE KONKANI FOLK-LORE TALES.

RAVALO SHENAI AND HIS SHREW OF A WIFE

Nobody considers himself happy all the time. There is always more or less a big fly in life's ointment. Ravalo Shenai had the misfortune to have the biggest fly. His wife was that fly that drove away all thoughts of a happy comfortable existence. Ravalo Shenai considered himself the most wretched man in this world. All that because his wife was a shrew of first water. If the lady—her name was Indiri was asked to do one thing, she was sure to do something quite opposite. She used to take particular delight in going against her husband in season and out of season. Nothing abashed her. No wonder that none of her neighbours loved her. And she returned the compliment. Indiri regarded her husband as a sort of black beetle and despised him.

Ravalo Shenai had a sweet tooth. His wife was fully cognisant of it. That is why he could not get any sweet dishes from one year's end to the other. Ravalo developed a desire for custard. But to desire one thing and to get it, were two different things. Once or twice, he tried to turn the talk to custard, jellies and so on. But the wife stopped all that non-sense and asked her husband to think of his work and the shortness in money for household expenses. You are a worm, a loafer, a shiftless back-boneless disgrace to humanity," cried the irate wife to her husband. "You think of custard, while I have been working my bones off, from morn till night to feed you—you brute." Bai Indiri turned perfectly pale with rage and it was only the exhaustion that stopped that torrent of invectives against her husband.

The desire grew. The hankering got intense. Ravalo dreamt of that custard. He slept over the thought of that custard—only to awaken when he found that even in his dreams that dish of custard was snatched away by some-body who looked like his better half. Ravalo lost all reason. He gave up his work. He had a vision of big dishes of custard floating before him. He lost his taste for food. His condition was made worse because he dared not open his lips for that custard. His wife's strident notes vibrated like a streak of lightning through his brain. He lost sleep. His ribs asserted themselves into prominence.

Ravalo came across one day, his neighbour's wife who was a kindly old soul. What is the matter with you, my old friend Ravalo ? What has squeezed out your bowels, you scare-crow ! The kindly touch, the sympathetic voice, acted as a sort of Bromide and made Ravalo open his heart to the old lady. Custard or rather the want of it, has been the disease that has been sapping my strength. You know the tragedy of my life. "I want that custard. There is the ache of emptiness all throughout me for that custard." "Don't you lose heart—you great baby. There is a way and a simple way of getting that custard, Don't you be down-hearted. Invite your brother-in-law, your wife's brother for dinner one day. But see that you insist that your wife should prepare every sweet dish except that custard. Tell her that since the last talk, you had become nauseated with the very name of that custard. So pray to her, not to go in for custard. And you will have that custard." Well, the plot succeeded. The brother-in-law turned up. And Indirabai went out of her way to cook a good sized dish of custard, simply because her " Lord and Master " had shown an abhorrence for it. Both the husband and her brother sat down to their meals. Good orthodox Brahmins are always careful to recite their prayers before partaking of their meals. And

Ravalo and his brother-in-law were no exceptions. The wife served a good dishful to her brother and was going to put in, a good quantity before her husband, simply because he did not like it. But the sight of that sweet custard, filling his eyes and his nostrils spread a joyous blaze in his features. The wife marked it and understood it and quietly turned away putting a spoonful or two before her husband. But the latter was equal to the occasion. He asked his brother-in-law to throw away carefully the water with which the prayers were performed into the pot in which a Tulsi plant was planted and during his temporary absence, he changed the dishes quietly putting before himself the dish which contained a good substantial quantity of the custard. His wife saw too late what had happened but could not help it. She went into a side room and showed a good sized stick to her husband which told him what to expect. The dinner went on and the husband was actually starved. It was bed-time. The wife prepared a nice soft bedding for her brother and asked her husband to make himself comfortable on a rough blanket or two. The brother-in-law was restless and could not get any sleep. His stomach was too full. Ravalo asked him to come down to his rough bed as the special bedding was too full of bugs. So they changed beds. Ravalo made himself comfortable on tho soft cushions and waited developments. After an hour or so, the brother-in-law got up howling. There was a noise of a good sized stick falling on his body. His cries were terrible. He ran away and the noise suddenly ceased. Ravalo went to his brother-in-law, quieted him and asked him why he groaned like that. I was thrashed with a lathi, articulated the poor brother-in-law. "Bosh"! said Ravalo. "Your heavy stomach must have caused you to go in for dreams. You better come back to your soft bed." "My body is aching" exclaimed the brother-in law. No more sleep for me. Don't you be nervous, you fool! Let me massage your body and you will feel comfortable. In a few minutes, the brother-in-law fell into a disturbed sleep and Ravalo laid himself down on the blankets.

Bai Indirabai was simply blazing with anger. The castigation which she wanted to administer to her beloved spouse, had fallen on wrong shoulders. Her eyes simply burnt with hatred. She trembled with passion. My husband's turn now, she said to herself. An hour passed. She did not know that they had changed beds again. Thinking that her husband was lying on the soft bed, she used the stick with such a concentrated hatred as to break a good many bones of her own brother. There was a terrible howling but the beating went on till the poor helpless brother-in-law became unconscious. Indirabai quietly stole back to her inner room. She went to sleep with an easy mind, fully believing that she had laid her husband low for some months to come. What a happy wife!

The hubbub, the cries had disturbed the neighbours. They came flocking in. Lamps were lighted and the poor brother-in-law was brought back to consciousness by the unremitting efforts of the neighbours, especially the old lady, who had advised Ravalo on the first occasion. Bai Indirabai had to come out of her room and fell down into a swoon when she found that on both the occasions, she had beaten her own brother. Nobody attended to her.

Who gave the beating—was the question asked on all sides. No satisfactory answer was forthcoming. As no sacrificial offerings were made, for some time past, to the ghosts living in the big peepal tree in the compound, it was thought that the ghosts must have exercised their vengeance on the guest of the day. The old lady winked. She was too clever for this sort of superstition. She called Ravalo on one side and advised him to take his brother-in-law to his village straight off. She asked him particularly to stay there, at his brother-in-law's house till his wounds got well. Even then, it was a question whether Ravalo should or should not come back to his wife. Had I been in your position, my friend Ravalo, said the wise lady, I would have started on a long pilgrimage to the Holy places. That would wash away the sins committed by you, in your former lives. These sins alone must have made it possible for the Goddess Fate to entangle your life's destiny to this virago Indirabai of yours. Wherever you go and stay, that is your home. Wherever you find peace and tranquillity, rest assured that is the home and *that* will be blessed by our Gods. The Sanskrit poet says :—

शय्या भूमितलं दिशोऽपि वसनं ज्ञानामृतं भोजन ।
मेते यस्य कुटुम्बिनो वद सखे कस्माद् भयं योगिनः ॥

One does not know whether the wise old lady had read her Emerson, who repeats in similar strains.

" Go where he will, the wise man is at home,
" His hearth, the earth ; his hall, the azure dome.
" Where his clear spirit leads him, there's his road,
" By God's own light illumined and fore-shadowed.